HIDDEN
DOORWAYS
AND SMALL ESCAPES

POEMS BY Magi Discoe

Cover Photo: Romany McNamara

ISBN (Print): 978-1-09838-286-5
ISBN (eBook): 978-1-09838-287-2

Table of Contents

The poet who overcharges for a poem shall be
stripped of half his rank in society.

FROM BREHON LAW, 6TH CENTURY

Borrowed Babies

A sacred day.
A new being exists.
The infinite elects the finite.

And, choosing form,
she embraces the
snare.

Emerging from soft darkness, she lifts her
sleepy lids and enters the wondrous,
painful light.

Eyes open, she divides the
shadows, splinters the
universe.

No longer floating in her silken web, she feels
the pull of the earth forcing her down into
her mother's arms.

"She's alert, she looked at me.
She is beautiful, an old soul."
Expectations abound.

For her, a hazy circle, a loud, bright new world.
I fear for her,
that we will think she is ours, forget
we are only the caretakers of our
beautiful, borrowed babies.

The Miraculous Hotel

Inside the mirror, a miraculous hotel,
And within resides the multitude,
The many travelers, true and fell.

The young, the innocent, the cruel and kind,
The wise, the fearful and courageous
All through the portcullis climb.

And each believes she's special, separate and unique.
But there is one who knows the world is whole
And there is nothing there to seek.

And when the joists begin to crumble and the siding shifts
The once elegant façade loosens, dissolves, and slips.

But who looks out the window and who is there to tell?
When the final roof beam breaks in the miraculous hotel?

2013

Autumn

November's dark curtain
Lifts late.
Summer's soaring sun now
Slips over the eastern edge slowly.
And sliding slow, slants south.
As we huddle in dark houses
Autumn's golden glow recedes,
And we face the blacks and whites of winter.

—For Autumn (1969-2010)

Chum

Cruising the deep, cold waters,
Silent sharks glide,
Even in sleep they move.
The constant movement washes
Pink gills, pulsing life and breath.

In the hour of the black dog,
Small fingers flying,
A large man, cold and pitiless,
Chums the roiling waters.
Chums the roiling waters.

2016

The Interpreter

My ears are full of hearing aids,
My eyes behind glass,
Teeth of gold,
Shoulders of titanium.
I am destined to interact
With the world through an interpreter.
My "real self"
Would be dead by now.

2019

Learning to Dance

She (the young woman) has taken up dancing.
Dance is her mother's delight, and her mother is pleased at this.
The daughter focuses on swing,
The mother favors waltz, rumba, samba, and also some swing.

The daughter tells me about it.
The dancing, I mean.
I say, "Ah, like your mom."
She says, "I don't like to hear that." I didn't either, about my mother,
Nor does my daughter, about me.

Mothers and daughters,
Dance partners from the first step.
Mothers' arms stretch in welcome and encouragement of
The daughter's early dance, graceless and exquisite.

Mothers and daughters,
So connected, we struggle to separate.
And just when we relax, daughters and mothers, just at the
good distance,
The genetic rubber band snaps back
To strike again that tender aching place.
When the band contracts
We spiral into our great fear,
The thing we hide from in the mirror, Becoming Her, our mother.
Our flawed, blemished, imperfect mother.

Afraid, we retreat,

Only to fall back in again.

For if the band breaks, we are set adrift,

Unconnected to the generations before us,

The chance to integrate and understand lost forever.

Still we hope

That no matter how hard the pull or push,

No matter how stretched the rubber band,

How painful the reunion,

Some day we may see our own clear reflection, dancing in the mirror.

For Leeza and Olga, 2018

Salmon Girl

Little Fish,
Salmon Girl
Grows restless
In a shallow stream

Senses sounds of wider waters
Senses cold and black unfolding
Longs to see into that blackness,
Feel that cold upon her tongue.

She turns in her sleep
Blinks away her child eyes
To see the ocean's vastness
And on her every golden scale gleams the light of the sea

In glorious abandon she flashes
Makes a leap and joins the current,
Hooked mouth, strong and swift she swims
"Little Salmon," the great water rejoices.

And she begins her fated journey
Leaving birth and death
For the deep water
To learn the mind of the sea.

Solstice, 1999

Music at School

2G hallway, tightly-packed, slow-moving, no echo left of 2nd bell.
Slapping hands, calling loud loud,
Pushing, standing, being cool, watching.

Slapping out a rhythm in syncopated time,
it starts easy,
the singing.

Voices venture and retreat, scaffold,
rising and weaving the sound,
the singing building, moving, louder,
drowning out the lessons,
the chemistry, the physics,

'Til a door opens and a shrill voice cries,
"I can't hear myself teach."

2000

Wild Plums

The wild plums are ripe in the lower vineyard.
The red ones are delicious,
But the yellow ones are sweeter.
All the animals have loose stool.

Spring 2004

Time

Time, no longer an endless horizon,
At fifty becomes finite.
In the morning, the body agrees,
Slow on the descending staircase. Knees nod their support.

And no more ruby moons
To proclaim her the center of creation
Marking month by month
Her missed chance at immortality

Now she slips through the streets,
A small wind disturbing only the most loose of leaves.
She is released
From her life among the predators of youth and age.
She is released
To sweep unhindered down among blind eyes.

1996

Early Morning Awakening at Vedanta Retreat

Sitting in silence
She looks across the dark meadow.
The rain has stopped.
Water, dense and flat, stands in ruts and small puddles.

Along the ridge, what yesterday were trees
Could be mountains, grass, or a black carpet.
This is the world of the beginning,
Before the existence of color.

She merges into this moment,
Enfolds and is enfolded
Into the moment of the beginning of color,
The moment of the new bright green day.

The pines across the meadow turn
from grey to dark green
And the grass slowly rises from her black sleep.
When was the moment when all began to change and puddles
became diamonds?

And suddenly, everywhere there appear diamonds.
They drip from foggy railings and wink from grass.
They shine, gold and red and green
At the turn of a head.

The brilliance of water.
The transformation of the world.
This is the world of the beginning,
The beginning of color
In the beauty of light.

For Sister 2019

The Nature of Geese

The two Graylag geese
Have been causing problems again,
Attacking the cars
On Graton Road.

Consumed with terrible ferocity
They hold back nothing, and
With a horrid screech, they charge.

The car horns blast.
Brakes screech and cars stop.
The geese waddle away, dignified and arrogant,
Assured once more of their power.

2006

Relief from Stillness

Suddenly time opened like a cartoon door hiding a precipice,
The one where Wiley Coyote comes storming through… looks down
Onto nothingness, blue sky beneath, above, around
A step across the empty doorway into the void.

Just yesterday, time rested in cramped baskets.
Errands, routines, small jobs, and duties jostling for recognition
Like red-mouthed baby birds.
Now, neglected post-it notes in carnival colors obsolesce on her
computer screen.

Ignored are life's lesser obligations,
Those hedges against day-to-day emptiness.
Extending an arm becomes a surprising effort
Against a tyranny of distance. She is unarmed.

Innumerable small tasks go undone
For hours extending into days
Days extending into weeks, weeks into months.
Focus diminishes to the pulling up of pants,
the arranging of bed covers.

Time, once so packed, sprawls
Spacious and vast.
Stillness brings relief from pain.
Reaching for a cup becomes mindful.
Each small action is considered.
Each movement is debated,

Rejected or accepted in
A new economy of need.

2016

Farewell Two Arms

I loved you,
I thought we would never part.
You were the source of my gentle caresses
Of warmth when you crossed my chest.
You pulled inward to pray, pushed outward to curse.

You raised yourselves to cheer.
Discouraged, you hunched and receded.
We knew each other, my arms.
And now, cold metal rests in your hallowed place.

I wanted to keep you,
A memento, a keepsake of our lifetime love.
With merciless hygiene, they refused: "Body parts must not leave
the hospital."
Now, we are parted forever.
The pain of our parting is with me still.

 —Post shoulder surgery, 2017

On the Death of Our Friend

Our Friends
Here, not here.
Life, too,
Is sudden.

—To Bob, 1994

The Ninth Fish

Eight fish.
The boy leans forward looking down.
Shapes deep in the waters,
Flash of a golden scale.

He dreams about the mysteries
Of these flashing fish
As in twos and threes they
Glide just below the surface.

Yet, the deeper mystery
Is the ninth fish
For whom we must look upward
From the infinite waters
Of the sacred stream.

By this, we are reminded,
That the last view is upward,
And we see the ninth fish
From beneath the waters of the stream.

2009

Seagulls

July again.
Seagulls, orange-lipped dowagers,
Charge the waves
In raucous confusion,
Then rise in graceful gangs
Unsatisfied,
Furiously reproaching
The sustaining winds.

Winter Poem

In winter, the sky gods appear,
Witnessing Spring's hopes nestled in the crooks of barren trees.
The secret places are now revealed to all, stark clumps of tumbled
twigs on windswept branches.

Wind and rain
Reap soft summer's greenness
And the gray stalks glisten
As the land lays open beneath a white sky.

Sleeping turtles, snakes and bears
Return to the earth gods,
Gods resting under muddy waters,
And white snow.

In the winter's bareness
The unburdened earth whispers
And the sky gods
Move through the openness.

Pictures

My Father was his mother's boy, handsome and glib,
a wild man with a trophy scrapbook, leather-bound
(courtesy of the Navy).
Hat set at an angle, tight, white sailor pants and shirt,
he sits with dark-skinned girls on his lap, nuzzling his cheek against
a background of painted palms.
In another picture, he walks with another young girl, his arm locked
around her neck.
She seems to enjoy it.
On each page a different scene, a different girl.
My mother stands in the middle
Of a large Irish family, twelve children, selling bread in the
Great Depression.
Ten years later, she has joined the Navy. She has become a nurse,
helping the shattered and healing, the wounded of WWII.
In the last year of war, my stout mother was struck by scarlet fever.
We see her two months later, slender,
with black, black hair tucked under a hard-starched nurse's cap.
A fat baby eats soap in a bassinette next to a trailer.
In the next picture, I am a year old and two older brothers
have appeared.
We laugh in our identical cowboy shirts.

My grandmother, pink and floral, smiles in the background.

Five years later, we eat ice cream together.

Mine dribbles down my coat as my brother wipes my mouth.

A year later, the pictures are only of me.

My grandmother beams at my father almost coyly,

My mother is slightly turned from the camera. The boys are gone.

In my fourteenth year, my cousin Linda comes to live with us

direct from Uncle Henry on the orphan shuffle.

We hide beer under a blanket in the closet.

Now we are standing in my grandmother's living room,

dressed for a junior prom and uncomfortable in too tight dresses on

chubby bodies; we don't know where to put our hands.

There are no more pictures of my father and Linda, nor of the rumpled

sheets, nor of my mother, running, screaming down the center of our

quiet suburban street.

A big wedding.

The bridesmaids are lined up in long teal dresses,

breasts hard and pointy.

Linda looks pretty good in a long, lacy, white dress.

Her husband Ed is older, stooped, with a large Adam's apple.

My grandmother looks relieved.

My mother and father are not there. The wedding looks expensive.

By the next year, my mother has moved out,

back to her Massachusetts sisters.

No one is taking pictures across 3,000 miles. An angry silence.

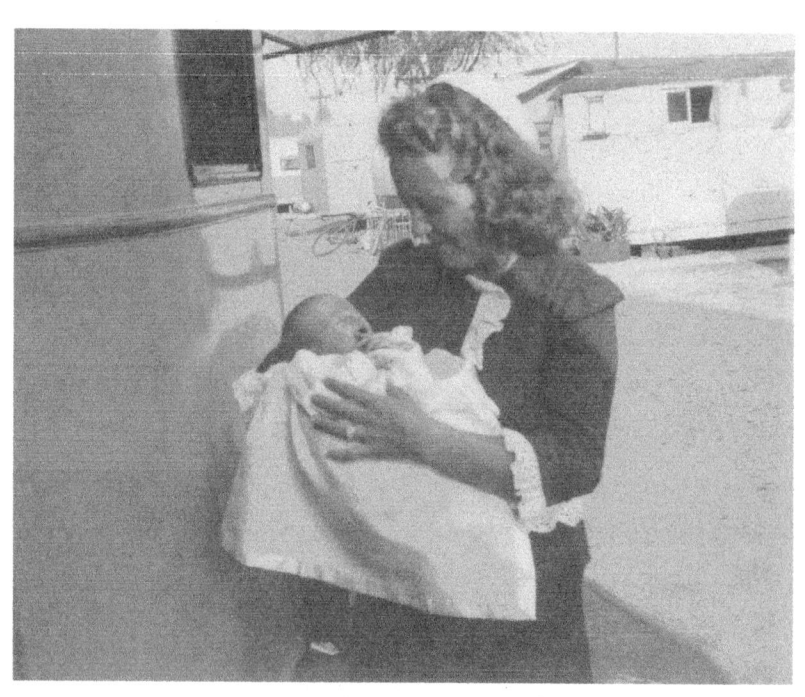

"I kiss your cheek and am engulfed by the warmth of your tenderness,"
it rhapsodizes.

"I didn't know if it was ok to give you this card," signed "Dad".

That night I stuff my clothes into old Safeway bags and head out.

Mother has returned.

In the photograph, she sits on the living room couch. Her hair is
now blond, and stoutness has morphed into an impressive belly,
incongruous above slender, attractive legs.

Beside her is a glass of whiskey,

One of many.

She wears a pink, nylon, quilted robe.

It looks to be about one o'clock in the afternoon.

I am looking at death certificates.

My father's: terminal emphysema.

Mother's is still pending thirty years later to permit burial in hallowed
Catholic earth.

I am standing cradling my child in my arms. My head is tilted, and my
hair falls toward the baby who idly catches it in a fat fist.

My eyes and mouth smile in a burst of hope and love.

I am reminded of an earlier picture of a mother holding her child

Her head tilts, and black, black hair falls toward the baby,

who idly catches it in a fat fist;

Her eyes and mouth smile in a burst of hope and love.

Beloved of Zeus

Beloved of Zeus—how would that be?
Held safe from Hera's scrutiny.
If Zeus's spirit coalesced
And stiffened to a rosy breast.

And if foreseeing Zeus' ride,
I behind a fern did hide,
And if in pleasure to rejoice,
What bird or beast would be my choice?

In all his rich philandering
He appeared to maids as many things.
His subtle skill to change his shape
To some might constitute a rape.

But what did Leda really cry
When those smooth feathers pressed her thigh? And what did Europa
really beg, As velvet nostrils warmed her leg?

But what's the use of all this license,
If after pleasure, there is silence?
And we implore him to turn back again,
To forms more commonly employed by men?

Deception can the loins ignite
And change of form produce delight
But other methods may suffice.

Helleborus

Startled by a phrase,
Grief opened like a flower.
The dormant seed,
Planted long ago in a dark moment,
Broke the surface and put forth buds.

Beautiful Helleborus,
Lethal bloom that
blossoms in the barren fields,
Hangs in hallowed flower clusters,
Bright against the winter's grays.

The blind gardener of my early nights
Seeded these fields where now I move
Amid the palmate leaves,
Among the hardy sepals masked as petals

And as I walk by this old footpath
The perennial seed
Planted in that bleak youth
Blooms again and I pause my slowed step in wonder at my
youth's flower.

Banging on the Doorway of Compassion

Banging on the doorway of compassion,
I like to think a miracle can happen—
That the door will swing, and open wide,
And, reaching out, I'll be inside.

It might be Karmic intervention,
Sunspots, ions, fluid retention,
But no matter how I push and shout,
The door stays shut, and I stay out.

So, to succeed in my endeavor,
I need a method far more clever,
And I hear rumors of techniques
That will provide me what I seek.

Some say the heat of my desire
Could set compassion's door on fire,
And I and door ignite at last
Free from future, free from past.

Others claim through observation,
Attention and determination,
I'll enter through small cracks and seams
And slip outside this land of dreams.

An entourage led by a saint
Might help me penetrate the gate;
And following a guru's whim,
If asked, I'd just say, "I'm with him."

And the truth of this is known quite well,
That separate egos tend to swell,
Making access through that door
An even more preposterous chore.

An ego slimming exercise
Could be of use, and well-advised.
And knowing death will be my fate
Will certainly reduce that weight.

If all this fails, then quiet time
To reach inside my monkey mind,
To dive, to swim in deeper seas
No thought of yous and thems and mes.

The Moon and the Sea

The green seas awakened the moon.
Black salt in her veins,
She sang to him
Implored him to linger, as he turned his face full.

Ripples penetrated the darkness,
Seeking remote caverns,
Wrenching the most distant sands
As she rose to him.

In the silent depths, neon fish rolled,
Twisted and turned in her endless mass,
And she trembled sending waves to engulf the shore.

And she flowed to him
And she serenaded him with the winds
And, keening, the gulls too were drawn up
As all her thousand parts rose to him.

He would turn again,
And she receded,
Waiting for the turning of the tides,
Leaving sea creatures gasping in the darkness of the shore.

Waiting

My belly ripens with memories of warm sands.
My lover wanders along the grey North Sea shore.

Separate as birds and united by the sea?

The gull's cry echoes only the wind.
A silver shape flashes through an ancient ocean.

Silently, we await the tides that will bring her to the shore.
Enfolded in separate joys, we dream
While the voice of the sea deafens us, screaming softly in a
brittle pink shell.

1979

June 4, 1979

Pink and fierce,
You roared against the thunder.
Fists clinched,
You inhaled the world.
Spirit of the winds that rolled from Africa,
You chose form
And I was your accomplice,
In those dry days.
Daughter of night,
Long-legged Artemis,
Pursuer of thoughts,
Stomper and dancer.

1980

Wolf Boy

Man-child of wolves
whose cries echo through mountains,
You step silently as snow
In the home of the dead.

They saw the silent wolf in you,
Brought you to the pack,
Revealed to you the magic circle,
The eaters of souls, the breeders of anger.

Sacrifice to the wolf god,
Wanderer through a thousand midnights,
Witness to a thousand shadows,
You are the hunter and the hunted in the mute kingdom.

Father of the stolen child,
Searching through winter rains,
Serenaded by distant baying.

1992

Love Poem

With the unhurried touch of the blind, we love.

Without the name
We sort the thousand forms.
We offer, retreat.

Blind fish in a black sea,
Moles, we burrow in.

Reaching forward,
We caress the unknown beast.

The Puppet Master

The puppet master knows his stuff,
His fingers fast and sure.
Each thread he pulls, each reposition moves,
and then its path obscures.

His touch is slight, just barely felt,
He weaves his web so fine
Each moment free within its range
But tight enough to bind.

The puppet master's hard to find.
He works behind the scenes.
He cares not if you're black or white,
Not burdened by your dreams.

Your mouth may move, but not your hands,
You may live with whom you please
But you will never own the land
And the master holds the keys.

1972

The Night Rower

The night rower
Glides across the black water.
Silver fish light the path.
And this night there is no moon,
Only the black water.
She sings, hands holding on the smooth oars.
Tonight, a warm breeze
Licks across her smooth skin
In this the soft night.
She rows naked,
A tiny seed in the great palm of darkness,
Moving across the vast and open seas.
The back arches, the arms pull,
The legs extend,
Again, again, again.
The small boat slips through water. And, cradled, she glides gently,
Rocked by the great westerlies.
And naked, she rows through the diamond night,
Moving spoonfuls of water in the vast and endless sea.

2017

Throwing Pebbles Down a Well

We do not see the white magnolia blossoms
But only their echo
In the dance of photons.
Our knowledge of life is indirect.
We see only reflection,
Each moment a vision of the past.
The belligerent jay, the melodious warbler
are disturbances in the air until
The push of sound that makes the eardrum tremble,
The soft cat curling at our feet,
The dog's wet tongue,
We know only secondhand, a message transferred by molecules
And so it is with you, my love,
I speak to you with pebbles
Thrown down a bottomless well.

2021

Prayer to Ease Dying

Let fear fly through me,
Taking with it the weight of my heart.

Let light fly into me
Illuminating all the places held in darkness.

Let my breath be the wind that carries
Me across the sky.*

*"Sometimes I go about in pity for myself, and all the while,
A great wind is carrying me across the sky."
An Ojibwe saying

Comments on Poems

*Borrowed Babies

Our children's lives will be different from ours, and in some ways, they may mesh with us, and some become estranged. We would like to have the power to lead them to what we feel is the right path, but as they grow and mature, they may choose to enter passageways that are unknown to us, and enter some that are against our deepest desires.

Miraculous Hotel

Who do we see when we look into a mirror? It is certainly not the same person we saw ten years ago, 20 years ago or even yesterday. These selves change from moment to moment, year by year, both internally and externally. Subjectively, our vision does not include our visage, only a wide view encompassing the world. Douglas Harding, an English mystic-philosopher and author of "*On Having No Head*", has said "only a fuzzy cloud where we have been told our nose should reside." So, who is it who is looking and who has been for so many years?

I am reminded of one of my favorite Haikus:

> Now that my storehouse
> Has burned down, nothing
> Conceals the moon
> > Masahide death poem, 1723

Autumn

Autumn and her daughter were students of mine. They came together to enjoy learning science. One day, I went to we deliver a rocket to Autumn and was told she had died the day before. Suddenly, no reason. She was so young and vibrant, and she and her daughter were so exciting to teach. I wrote this poem soon after her death.

2010 For Autumn

Chum

How riled up we are. How devastating our politics, how chaotic. The news, our leaders, our press, ourselves, smell the blood. While the media pimps of despair circle and snap for leftovers: the chum. 2018

The Interpreter

Hearing aids, artificial joints, glasses, are all the paraphernalia of aging for the privileged in our country. Inhalers keep us breathing, medications keep our blood pressure low, our gluttony is eased by insulin. Thru these interventions, we interpret the world.

Learning to Dance

My fear of becoming like my mother was triggered by a chance remark from a friend. Her mother has been a long-time ballroom dancer and recently, my friend, the daughter, has also taken up dancing. When I became a mother myself, I began to understand the complexities of the relationship. My own mother had died many years before, so I never had the opportunity to explore this with her. It was serendipitous that my friend asked me if things she said would ever be in a poem—say, poem #22. I originally titled this poem #22.

Salmon Girl

This was written for my daughter, who I knew would head for the sea as soon as she was able to. I had raised her to find her independence, and as she moved away and into her own life, I found it both marvelous and painful.

Wild Plums

My husband and I once lived in an idyllic vineyard surrounded by wild plum trees. During the fall, we would see the flattened animal scat full of the pits of those delicious plums.

Time

As I grow old, I watch myself become, as most old ladies become, invisible. This has been both a blessing and a curse.

The Nature of Geese

In this same vineyard, two domestic white geese (no doubt escaped from some farm) lived on a farm pond across the road. They chose to make their nest down a small incline very close to the road. In the mornings, we would hear cursing, the blaring of car horns and the cacophony of angry geese. As good Samaritans, we and our nearest neighbor herded them up and under and around the vines crisscrossing the vineyard to a safer pond. They inevitably returned to their spot by the road, and the morning ritual started again. They remained ungrateful.

Relief from Stillness

One year I had two complete shoulder replacement surgeries. For months, I was unable to lift a full cup or bring a book to my lap. There was no escape from my confinement. The only thing to do was to go meet it.

Farewell Two Arms

In shoulder replacement, the surgeon cuts through the humerus. The top of the humerus is replaced with a titanium insert, which is inserted into the shaft. I guess they just destroy the bones. They would not let me have them back. I'm not sure what I would have done with them anyway.

On the Death of our Friend

No matter how long ago our friend died, the feeling of loss pierces us unpredictably. Those sudden moments bring to my attention that our moments of being awake and alive also happen with sudden revelation.

The Ninth Fish

I gave my husband a brass Chinese brush holder for his birthday. Wrapping around that brush holder, fish are displayed in animated relief. All the fish dive except for one.

Seagulls

I have always loved the beauty and unapologetic irascibility of seagulls. They are eaters of garbage, thieves, and opportunists. Their glorious whiteness and soft feathers belie their cruel beaks.

Winter Poem

This was written the winter of 2005, but of course, it is also about the winter of my life, when the leafy trappings fall, and the core is revealed

Beloved of Zeus

What would it be like to make love with various animals? It's not like no one has ever thought of this before.

Helleborus

Helleborus are also called Lenten Rose because their beautiful and deadly blooms come in the dark of winter. In this poem, I remember the poisonous thoughts and habits I sowed when I was young, and as I age, I understand that these grow in me still.

Banging on the Doorway of Compassion

I have spent a great deal of my life exploring the concept of compassion. To me, compassion is not kindness, approval or feeling sorry for someone (although these feelings may be included). I believe compassion is understanding that you are not separate from the world. Thich Nhất Hanh, a Vietnamese Buddhist monk, uses the word "interbeing" and Douglas Harding describes "a vast emptiness that vastly filled, a nothing that found room for everything..."

This poem is a spoof the many attempts I have made to deeply understand what Buddhists call "compassion".

Waiting

My then husband and I traveled from the U.S. to the Netherlands. After working as laborers in the tomato greenhouses on Crete, where we separated, I left for Egypt while he left again for Holland. A month after coming to Alexandria, I realized I was pregnant. After a three-day wait to make a telephone call in Cairo, I was able to contact my husband in the Netherlands. We came together again in an uneasy truce.

Wolf Boy

This poem was written for a friend who was abused as a child. Those he trusted most betrayed him. Moving through and out of this, he found his own path. For all of us raised by wolves, there are faint tracks in the snow leading us to our own lives.

Love Poem

My husband and I met in our late 30s. At this age, we flung ourselves into passion, but remained more cautious about love. What we slowly created has lasted over 35 years and has granted us more love than either of us ever thought to hope for.

The Puppet Master

This poem arises from my fear and anger at being manipulated. It encompasses both the political and personal.

Throwing Pebbles Down a Well

For my daughter's entire life, she has guarded her feelings.She thinks carefully about things, but I am not often invited to the feast of thoughts. I was thinking about how much our understanding is dependent on feedback; from light entering our eyes, to compression waves entering our ear to bounce against the eardrum, moving tiny bones to create a wave in our cochlea. We throw a stone into a well. It is the echo, the response that gives us our understanding of the well.

Prayer to Ease Dying

On a silent retreat, I was in the meditation room and I felt my heart beating irregularly. I felt a fear I didn't expect. I tried to embrace it, imagining that I would die this very night. I wrote this as a kind of mantra to alleviate that fear.

Giving Thanks

To my husband Bob, for his many edits and unflagging support, love, and patience.

To all my friends from the Billy Collins Poetry and Pie group, for many years of gathering to read poetry aloud to one another. This practice has brought us joy, humor, insight and the extraordinary poetry which has opened our hearts to intimacy and compassion.

I especially want to thank Jim Shere, whose enthusiasm and gentle nudges have helped make this book a reality.

And to my daughter, Romany McNamara, who has led me to so many of these poems.